ALTERNATOR BOOKS™

THE MOON FILES

THE BIRTH OF THE MOON

Beth Adelman

Lerner Publications ◆ Minneapolis

Lerner Publications Company
An imprint of Lerner Publishing Group, Inc.
241 First Avenue North
Minneapolis, MN 55401 USA

For reading levels and more information, look up this title at www.lernerbooks.com.

Main body text set in Aptifer Sans LT Pro.
Typeface provided by Linotype.

Library of Congress Cataloging-in-Publication Data

Names: Adelman, Beth, author.
Title: The birth of the moon / Beth Adelman.
Description: Minneapolis, MN : Lerner Publications, [2025] | Series: The moon files (Alternator books) | Includes bibliographical references and index. | Audience: Ages 8–12 | Audience: Grades 4–6 | Summary: "Ever wonder where the Earth's moon came from? Readers will learn about the different theories people have offered throughout history. Then they will look at the latest information and evidence about the theories"—Provided by publisher.
Identifiers: LCCN 2023037060 (print) | LCCN 2023037061 (ebook) | ISBN 9798765625620 (library binding) | ISBN 9798765629789 (paperback) | ISBN 9798765637968 (epub)
Subjects: LCSH: Moon—Origin—Juvenile literature.
Classification: LCC QB582 .A337 2025 (print) | LCC QB582 (ebook) | DDC 523.3—dc23/eng/20231026

LC record available at https://lccn.loc.gov/2023037060
LC ebook record available at https://lccn.loc.gov/2023037061

Manufactured in the United States of America
1 – CG – 7/15/24

TABLE OF CONTENTS

The moon lights up Earth's night skies.

INTRODUCTION

THE MOON IS BORN

The moon is the biggest and brightest object in the night sky. It is also a great mystery.

No one knows for certain how the moon was formed. After all, no one was there to see it happen! Scientists must rely on theories to explain how it may have come to be. A theory is an idea about how and why something happened. Scientific theories are based on facts. Scientists work hard to prove their theories using evidence.

The Apollo space missions from 1968 to 1972 changed a lot of what we know about the moon. Scientists continue to learn about the moon using satellites, telescopes, spacecraft, computers, and other instruments.

The moon fills the human imagination with wonder. How was it born? What do scientists think happened after? Will we ever know for sure?

Astronaut Buzz Aldrin was one of the first humans to walk on the moon.

CHAPTER 1

ANCIENT STORIES

Ancient peoples looked up at the moon and wondered how it came to light up the dark night. They told stories about gods and animals and magical fires.

In a Finnish story, Ilmatar, daughter of the air, allowed a duck to lay eggs on her knee. The eggs fell. When they cracked, the whites became the moon and the yolks became the sun. The broken shells became the stars.

Finnish goddess Ilmatar was known as the "spirit of air."

According to Cree legend, one sibling was in charge of the sun and the other one was in charge of the moon.

The Cree, a First Nations people, live in western Canada. In their stories, the Creator kept the sun burning in the sky. When the Creator died, his son and daughter argued about who should keep up the fire. They argued so much that the sun nearly went out.

Wisakedjak, the sacred lawgiver of the Cree, decided the son would tend the fire during the day and the daughter would tend it at night. They would be separated across the sky because they argued so much.

Six Days of Creation

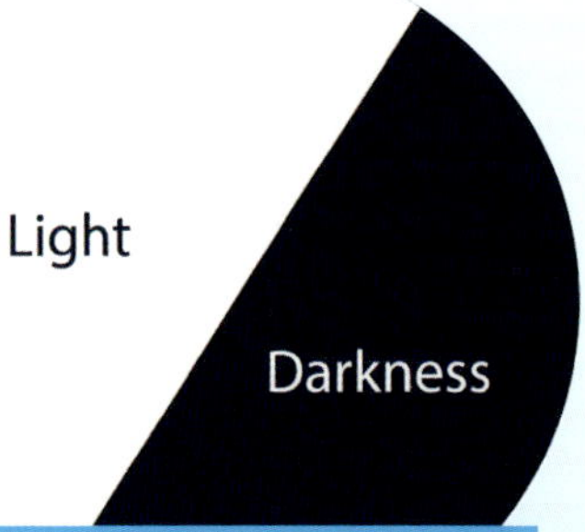

Day 1: Time, light, the heavens and Earth

Day 2: The sky and seas

Day 3: The dry land and plants

In creation, an all-powerful deity created the world in six days. The seventh day was for rest.

Day 4: The sun, moon, planets, and stars

Day 5: The fish and birds

Day 6: Land animals and humans

The Mystery of the Moon

In the Christian, Jewish, and Muslim faiths, everything on Earth and in space was made by a deity known as God, Yahweh, or Allah. He made the larger light, the sun, to rule the day. He made the lesser light, the moon, to rule the night. The creation process took six days. The moon, sun, and stars were made on the fourth day. The seventh day was for rest.

Stories of the Efik and Ibibio people of Nigeria said the sun and moon were husband and wife. Long ago they lived on Earth. One day their best friend, Flood, came to visit. Flood rose so high that the sun and moon had to sit up on the roof of their house. But Flood kept getting higher, and eventually the sun and moon had to leap into the sky.

In a Mongolian story, the beginning of all things was dark and silent. Esege Malan, the highest god, took a handful of earth, squeezed the moisture out of it, and made the sun. Then he took another handful and made the moon.

In Greek mythology, Selene was the moon goddess.

Scientists look for clues about the formation of our own solar system in star-forming regions.

CHAPTER 2

EARLY THEORIES

Scientists look at evidence to understand what happened in the past. When they look at our solar system, they have theories of how it began.

Evidence shows that our solar system may have formed about 4.5 billion years ago. The sun came first. It was formed from a giant spinning cloud of gas and dust called a nebula. The solar nebula got so big and heavy that its own gravity caused it to collapse. In the center of the flattened nebula was a new star: our sun.

These bits clumped together to form larger objects. One was Earth. Back then, the sun was much, much hotter than it is now. Earth was a red-hot ball of melted rock. It did not have a moon.

Rocks swirl around space to form a new planet.

A Rocky Start

So how did Earth get its moon? As early as the 1790s, some scientists believed that the solar system formed from a nebula. They thought that as debris started clumping together, the moon formed near Earth. Then Earth's gravity pulled the moon into orbit. This was called the Co-Formation Theory, because it said Earth and the moon formed in the same way.

By the late 1800s, scientists had learned more about how the gravity of the moon and Earth affect each other. Over time, the force of Earth's gravity has changed the orbit of the moon.

The Co-Formation Theory says that the solar system was formed from a nebula.

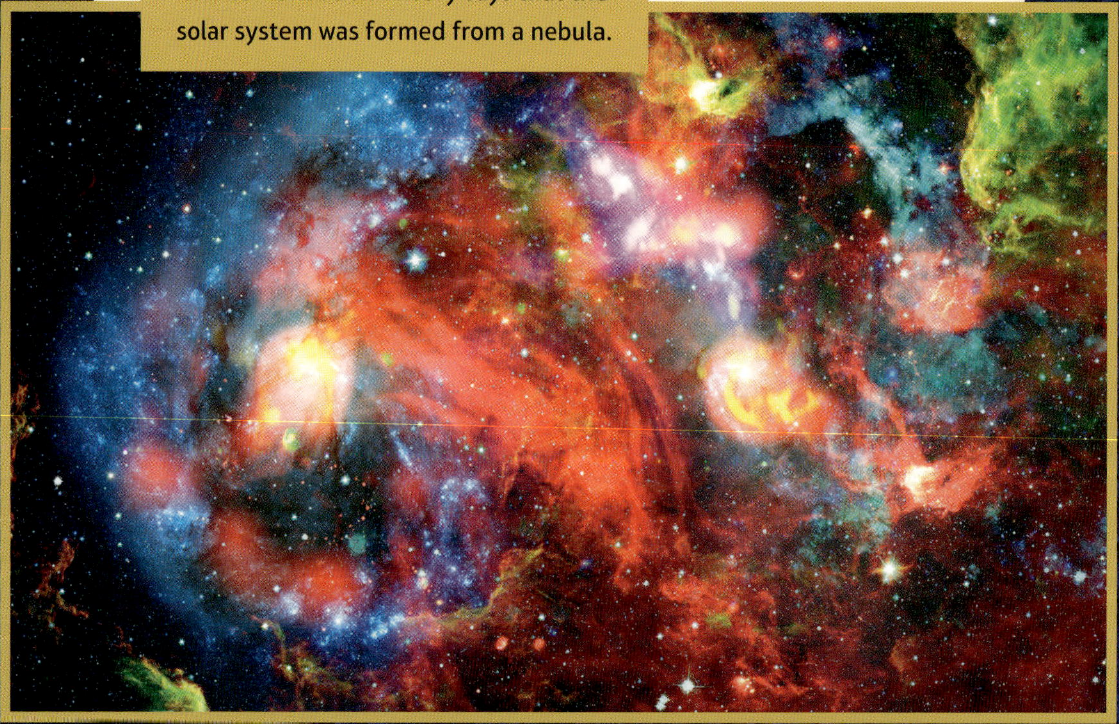

Earth was once a huge red ball of molten rock.

It has also made Earth spin slower than it did when the solar system formed.

Earth was a big ball of melted rock spinning really fast when the solar system formed. It's possible that a giant glob of liquid rock formed around the middle of Earth as it spun. The glob could have flung off, cooled, and then hardened into the moon. This was called the Fission Theory. "Fission" means splitting something into parts.

According to the Capture Theory, the Earth's gravity pulled the moon into its orbit.

Looking for Evidence

By the 1950s, many scientists had decided the Fission Theory was unlikely. Losing such a big glob of rock would have slowed down Earth's spin too much. But they had another idea—the Capture Theory.

The Capture Theory suggested that the moon was one of many large objects that formed when our solar system did. Back then, objects moved around in space. It took billions of years for them to settle into their orbits around the sun. The Capture Theory said that as the moon passed near Earth, the gravity of Earth pulled it into orbit.

Scientists spent a lot of time discussing the Co-Formation Theory and the Capture Theory. They needed evidence to find out which one was most likely.

Scientists know that Neptune's moon Triton is a captured moon because it is made up of different kinds of rocks.

Astronauts and scientists are still learning about the moon from rocks gathered during Apollo space missions.

CHAPTER 3

THE GIANT IMPACT THEORY

In 1969, the Apollo 11 moon mission brought back the very first rocks from the moon. When scientists studied them, they found evidence that did not agree with either of the two theories about how the moon was created. The moon rocks were much more like rocks on Earth than anyone expected.

This suggested a very different idea about how the moon was born. It's known as the Giant Impact Theory.

Different moons formed in different ways. They are not all made up of the same materials. Some moons have volcanoes. A few have atmospheres and even oceans beneath their surface. If there's life elsewhere in our solar system, scientists think it's most likely to be on a moon.

OTHER MOONS

Scientists have counted more than seven hundred and fifty moons in our solar system. Mercury and Venus are the only planets that do not have moons.

Venus does not have its own moon.

Scientists suggest that our moon was born when the planet Theia collided with Earth.

A New Idea

The Giant Impact Theory starts with the idea that lots of objects were still zipping through space in the early days of our solar system. These objects were big and small. Sometimes they crashed into each other.

One of those zooming objects may have been a planet named Theia, which was about the size of Mars. Earth and Theia crashed into each other. There was an enormous explosion. Theia was blown to bits.

Fast moving debris created chaos in space before our solar system came together.

Kaboom!

Theia and Earth were both made of red-hot liquid rock, and melted things combine more easily than solid things. So, some parts of Theia became part of Earth. Some parts of Theia were blasted out into space. Some parts of Earth were blasted into space as well.

The gravity of Earth pulled some of those blasted bits into clouds of debris. The clouds surrounded Earth. The debris clumped together into chunks of glowing hot melted rock. The chunks clumped together into bigger pieces, and then those pieces stuck together. At some point, all those pieces became the moon.

Billions of years ago, the moon was covered with oceans of red hot magma.

Basalt rock formed from cooled magma lava is found on the moon and on Earth.

The moon's surface is battered by hits from comets and asteroids.

Hot Stuff

For another 600 million years after the giant impact, crashes and collisions continued in the solar system. Large asteroids (small, rocky objects that orbit the sun) and comets smashed into the moon, creating heat. That heat melted the surface of the moon, forming an ocean of hot liquid rock called magma.

By about 3.8 billion years ago, there were fewer large objects moving around the solar system. The surface of the moon cooled and became solid. But smaller objects kept hitting the moon, making wide, deep craters.

In some places, the hot magma under the surface flowed up through cracks in the moon's crust, filling the craters. The magma hardened into a dark rock called basalt.

HIDDEN IMPACTS

Early in the life of our solar system, the moons and planets were struck by many big objects from space. The impacts created large craters on their surfaces. Earth is full of such craters. But plants, soil, and water hide most of them. Erosion and plate tectonics (the movement of the large, rocky plates that make up Earth's crust) also keep changing our planet's surface.

The Barringer Crater in Arizona is an example of an impact crater on Earth.

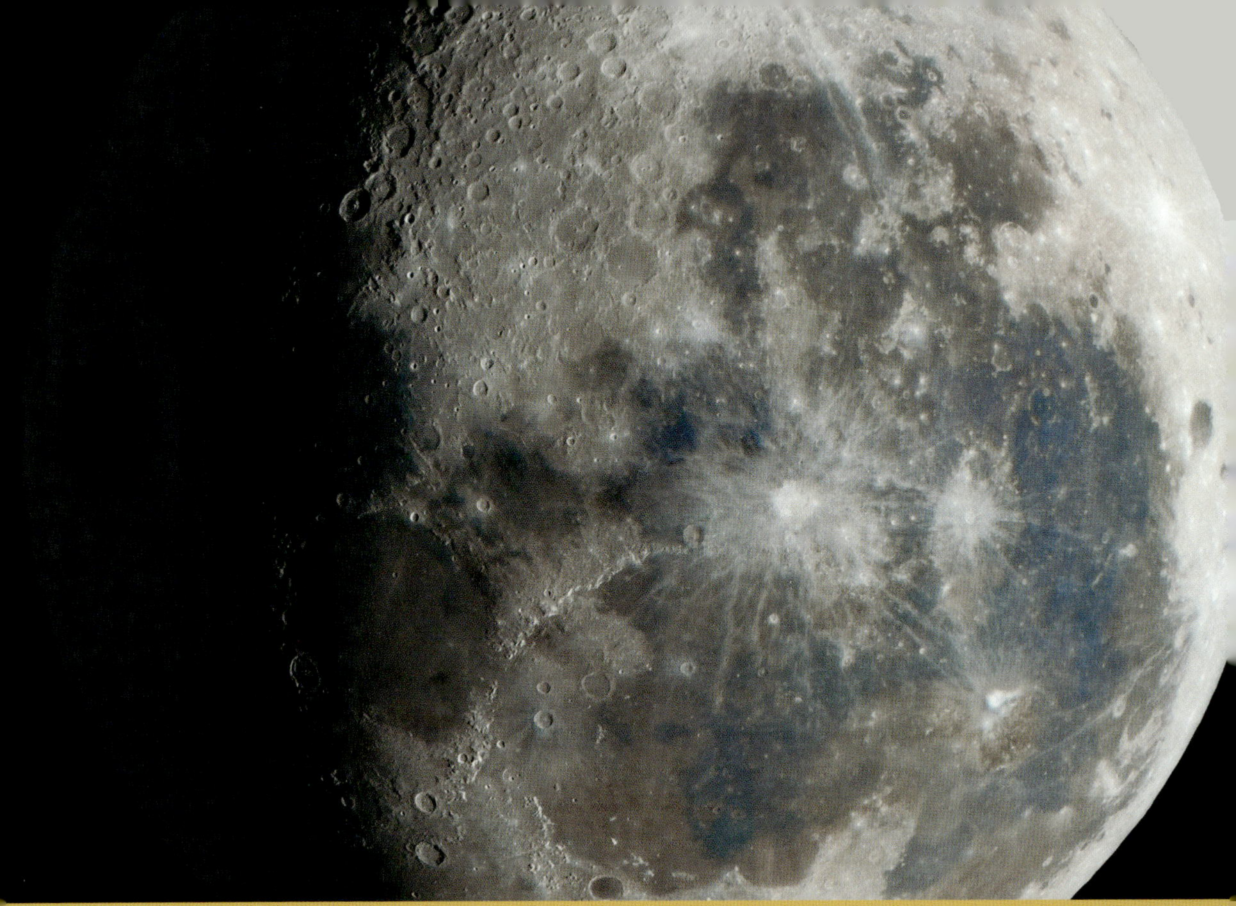

The moon's surface contains a variety of minerals that produce different colors in sunlight.

CHAPTER 4

EVIDENCE FOR THE GIANT IMPACT

A lot of the evidence for the Giant Impact Theory comes from the moon rocks the Apollo missions brought back to Earth. Minerals within rocks can tell us how a rock was formed and sometimes even how old it is.

The rocks revealed that the moon formed around 60 million years after the solar system began to take shape. The type of rocks showed that the moon was covered with a deep ocean of magma for at least tens of millions, if not hundreds of millions, of years. Scientists believe this is exactly what would happen after a giant impact: The energy released would melt almost everything.

Apollo 17 astronaut Harris Schmitt uses a lunar rake to collect small rock samples.

Rock Twins

The dark basalt rocks in the moon's craters are very similar to basalt rocks on Earth. Their minerals are the same. The sizes of the individual grains and crystals inside them are almost identical.

The forms of oxygen and other elements sealed inside the moon rocks are a close match to those on Earth. The basalt rocks are so similar that scientists are sure it can't just be a coincidence.

Certain elements vaporize (turn into a gas) when they are heated. Moon rocks contain only very small amounts of those elements. Scientists think a high-energy impact could have vaporized those elements off of the moon.

A moon rock gathered during the Apollo 17 mission sits on display in the Oval Office of President Joe Biden.

Five pieces of the moon were found on Earth by meteorite hunters during an expedition to Antarctica.

NASA scientists use complex computer models to explain the Giant Impact Theory.

A Space Story

Models created by a computer using all the evidence we have so far can also help scientists understand how the moon may have formed. They show how a huge collision, combined with gravity, could cause the moon and Earth to orbit and to spin the way they do.

Computer models also suggest that the moon originally formed much closer to our planet. Reflectors placed on the moon during the Apollo missions help us measure its distance from Earth. Those measurements show that the moon moves away from Earth by about 1.5 inches (3.8 cm) each year.

In 1984, scientists from around the world met to consider all the evidence. They decided the Giant Impact Theory is the most likely way our moon was born. But they keep studying the moon for more clues. The story of the moon's birth is the story of our solar system. It's the story of Earth, too.

Humans will always be curious about the moon and its origins.

GLOSSARY

atmosphere: mixtures of gases that surround Earth and some other planets

basalt: a kind of rock formed from rapidly cooling magma

crater: a huge, bowl-shaped dent found on the surface of an object

crust: the outermost layer on a planet or a moon

element: a pure substance, in solid, liquid, or gas form, made of one type of atom; building blocks of everything in the world

erosion: the process of being worn away by wind, water, and other natural forces

gravity: the force by which a planet or other body draws objects toward its center

magma: superhot melted rock below a moon or planet's crust; it becomes lava when it comes to the surface, and once it hardens it becomes basalt

orbit: a regular, repeating path that one object in space takes around another one

LEARN MORE

Adelman, Beth. *The History of Moon Exploration.* Minneapolis: Lerner Publications, 2025.

Britannica Kids: Moon
https://kids.britannica.com/students/article/Moon/275930

Hirsch, Rebecca E. *Mysteries of the Moon.* Minneapolis: Lerner Publications, 2021.

Huddleston, Emma. *Explore the Moon.* Minneapolis: Kids Core, an imprint of ABDO Publishing, 2022.

Lunar and Planetary Institute: Explore Marvel Moon
https://www.lpi.usra.edu/education/explore/marvelMoon

NASA Space Place: Moon
https://spaceplace.nasa.gov/search/moon

Rajczak, Michael. *Reaching the Moon.* New York: Gareth Stevens Publishing, 2021.

The Planetary Society: The Moon, Preserving Earth's Origin Story
https://www.planetary.org/worlds/the-moon

INDEX

PHOTO ACKNOWLEDGMENTS

Image Credits: interior background; HelenField/Shutterstock, interior background; TB3XNW/Alamy, interior background; titoOnz/Alamy, p. 4; Dani Caxete/NASA, p. 5; NASA, p. 6; Robert Wilhelm Ekman/Wikimedia Commons, p. 7; "Wesakechak and the Origin of the Moon", Acrylic on canvas, 2009, created by Lance Cardinal, Bigstone Cree Nation, Treaty 8 Territory, p. 8; Satina/Shutterstock, p. 9; Eroshka/Shutterstock, p. 10; ESA/Hubble/NASA, J. C. Tan (Chalmers University & University of Virginia), R. Fedriani (Chalmers University), p. 11; stevecoleimages/Shutterstock, p. 12; IvaFoto/Shutterstock, p. 13; Diego Barucco/Shutterstock, p. 14; Mopic/Shutterstock, p. 15; NASA, p. 16; Robert Markowitz/NASA, p. 17; NASA/Shutterstock, p. 18; Naeblys/Shutterstock, p. 19; sdecoret/Shutterstock, p. 20; NASA/SVS/GSFC, p. 21; Brester Irina/Shutterstock, p. 22; NASA, p. 23; turtix/Shutterstock, p. 24; astrovas/Shutterstock, p. 25; NASA, p. 26; NASA, p. 27; NASA, p. 28; metamorworks/Shutterstock, p. 29; FamVeld/Shutterstock.

Cover: Cover painting by William K. Hartmann/Planetary Science Institute